Veo 2 vs. OpenAI's Sora
Inside the World of AI Visuals

A Deep Dive into Google's VO2, ImageN 3, and the Future of Creativity

J. Andy Peters

Copyright ©**J. Andy Peters, *2024*.**

All rights reserved. No part of this publication may be reproduced, distributed, or transmitted in any form or by any means, including photocopying, recording, or other electronic or mechanical methods, without the prior written permission of the publisher, except in the case of brief quotations embodied in critical reviews and certain other noncommercial uses permitted by copyright law.

Table of Contents

Introduction...4
Chapter 1: The Rise of AI in Visual Storytelling......... 7
Chapter 2: Google's VO2 – A Game-Changer in AI Video.. 14
Chapter 3: ImageN 3 – Elevating AI-Generated Art. 27
Chapter 4: Whisk – A Creative Twist on Image Generation...33
Chapter 5: The Competitive Landscape................... 40
Chapter 6: Challenges and Limitations of AI Visual Tools.. 51
Chapter 7: The Future of AI Creativity...................... 59
Conclusion.. 67

Introduction

The world of creativity is undergoing a transformation unlike anything seen before. Artificial intelligence, once considered a tool for niche applications, has emerged as a powerful force capable of reshaping how content is imagined, designed, and brought to life. From filmmaking to digital art, marketing to experimental visuals, AI is not just enhancing creative processes—it's fundamentally redefining them. Its influence is growing at a pace that even seasoned industry veterans find both exhilarating and disorienting. The tools it offers are no longer just experimental novelties but essential companions for creators striving to push the boundaries of what's possible.

In this rapidly evolving landscape, the competition among AI-powered tools has become fierce. Companies like Google and OpenAI are leading the charge, vying for dominance in a market teeming with innovation and potential. Each has unveiled groundbreaking models that promise to revolutionize the way creators think about their craft. Google's suite of tools, including the cutting-edge VO2 for video generation, ImageN 3 for high-quality image creation, and Whisk for remixing visuals in entirely new ways, has positioned the tech giant as a formidable player. Meanwhile, OpenAI's Sora has captivated the imagination of many, showcasing AI's ability to generate intricate and mesmerizing video sequences from mere text prompts. These tools represent not just technological marvels but also a glimpse into the future of human creativity.

At the heart of this book lies a simple yet profound question: how are these innovations reshaping the creative landscape, and what does this mean for the future of art and storytelling? Google's offerings stand out for their focus on realism, cinematic quality, and accessibility, while OpenAI and other competitors bring their own unique strengths and challenges. Together, they are pushing the boundaries of what AI can do in ways that were once the stuff of science fiction.

This book aims to take you on a journey through this fascinating new world, delving deep into the mechanics, potential, and implications of AI-driven creativity. From the technical prowess of VO2 to the artistic flexibility of ImageN 3 and the playful experimentation of Whisk, we'll explore how these tools are shaping not just how we create, but also how we think about creativity itself. It's a story of innovation, rivalry, and the endless possibilities that emerge when technology and imagination collide.

Chapter 1: The Rise of AI in Visual Storytelling

The history of AI in creative industries is one of bold ambitions and incremental breakthroughs. In its early stages, AI-driven visuals were more of a curiosity than a credible tool. Developers experimented with rudimentary algorithms that could generate basic patterns or primitive animations, but the results were often crude and lacked any resemblance to professional-grade outputs. These early systems struggled to understand the complexities of human creativity—nuances like lighting, motion, and composition were far beyond their reach. AI-generated visuals felt artificial, limited by the technology's inability to grasp the subtleties of the real world.

One of the most significant hurdles was the lack of realistic physics and natural movement. Early models often produced animations where characters moved awkwardly, as if they were marionettes operated by invisible strings. Even when AI attempted static visuals, the results were riddled with errors, such as distorted faces or objects that seemed out of place. These limitations meant that AI-driven visuals were often dismissed as little more than an academic exercise, far removed from the demands of professional creators.

The breakthroughs began when AI models shifted from rule-based systems to machine learning and deep learning architectures. Instead of programming the AI with fixed instructions, developers began training models on massive datasets, allowing them to learn patterns and improve over time. This marked a turning point. By analyzing thousands—sometimes millions—of real-world images and videos, AI systems began to understand elements like texture, lighting, and motion in ways that were previously unattainable. With this foundation, AI could start generating visuals that were not only coherent but also visually compelling.

The arrival of generative adversarial networks (GANs) added another layer of sophistication. These networks pit two models against each other: one generates visuals, while the other evaluates their quality. Through this iterative process, AI could refine its outputs, making them more realistic with each cycle. Suddenly, the prospect of using AI for professional-grade visuals no longer seemed far-fetched.

These advancements paved the way for modern tools like Google's VO2 and OpenAI's Sora. Unlike their predecessors, these tools leverage state-of-the-art models that combine vast datasets with deep learning techniques to generate visuals that feel authentic and immersive. VO2, for example, incorporates an understanding of real-world physics, ensuring that movements and lighting behave naturally, while Sora focuses on transforming text prompts into visually stunning video sequences.

These tools didn't emerge overnight. They are the result of decades of experimentation, trial and error, and technological progress. Each breakthrough brought AI one step closer to where it stands today: not just a tool for hobbyists or researchers but a genuine game-changer for creators across industries. What was once an ambitious dream has become a reality, and the journey is far from over.

In a world where content is consumed at an unprecedented pace, the demand for faster, high-quality production has become relentless. From social media to streaming platforms, creators are under constant pressure to produce engaging visuals that capture attention and resonate with audiences. Traditional methods, while effective, often require significant time, resources, and expertise—barriers that can stifle creativity and exclude those without access to high-end tools or professional teams. This is where the promise of AI-driven visuals becomes transformative.

The ability of AI to generate realistic, high-quality content at a fraction of the time and cost represents a seismic shift in the creative process. Tools like Google's VO2 and ImageN 3 are designed to bridge the gap between aspiration and execution, enabling creators to bring their visions to life without the constraints of budget or technical expertise. These tools don't just speed up production; they open doors for a wider range of storytellers, from independent filmmakers to digital artists, who might otherwise struggle to compete in a saturated market.

More importantly, AI's potential to democratize creative production cannot be overstated. By simplifying complex workflows and automating repetitive tasks, AI empowers individuals who may lack traditional training or resources. A filmmaker with a vision but no access to expensive equipment can now use AI to simulate cinematic effects. An artist experimenting with new styles can rely on AI tools to generate variations and refine their work. This democratization ensures that creativity is no longer limited to those with privilege or institutional support; instead, it becomes accessible to anyone with an idea and the curiosity to explore.

The implications go beyond individual creators. Small businesses can produce professional-grade marketing materials without hiring a full design team. Educators can craft immersive visuals to enhance learning experiences. Even hobbyists can experiment with AI tools to express their ideas in ways that would have been unimaginable just a few years ago. By leveling the playing field, AI is redefining what it means to be creative in the modern era.

Yet, this is not just about convenience or cost-saving measures. AI-driven visuals represent a new frontier in artistic expression, pushing the boundaries of what can be imagined and achieved. As these tools continue to evolve, they are not just changing how content is made—they are challenging the very notion of who gets to create, making the world of visual storytelling richer, more diverse, and more inclusive than ever before.

Chapter 2: Google's VO2 – A Game-Changer in AI Video

At the core of Google's VO2 lies an extraordinary capability: the ability to generate visuals that mimic the intricacies of real-world physics. This is no small feat in the realm of AI, where earlier models often struggled to produce animations or videos that felt organic. Movements appeared stiff or robotic, lighting was flat and unrealistic, and the resulting visuals often felt more like simulations than creations. VO2 changes that by integrating a deep understanding of how objects, light, and motion interact in the physical world.

One of VO2's standout features is its ability to simulate natural movements with uncanny accuracy. Characters walking through a scene no longer move with awkward rigidity; instead, their strides have weight and rhythm, reflecting a clear comprehension of balance and momentum. Facial gestures, once plagued by over-exaggeration or uncanny stiffness, now carry subtlety and emotion, making AI-generated characters feel more lifelike. This leap in realism isn't just a technical achievement—it's a breakthrough for creators who rely on authenticity to tell compelling stories.

Lighting, too, receives a level of precision that elevates VO2 above its predecessors. By understanding how light interacts with surfaces, whether soft and diffused or sharp and direct, VO2 generates scenes that feel alive. Shadows fall naturally, reflections add depth, and subtle changes in light create an atmosphere that enhances the emotional impact of a scene. For creators, this attention to detail eliminates the need for painstaking post-production work, allowing them to focus on the story itself.

But where VO2 truly shines is in its focus on cinematic details, the kinds of elements that separate amateur visuals from professional-grade productions. It's not just about generating a scene—it's about capturing it with the finesse of a seasoned filmmaker. VO2 understands the language of cinematography, from lens effects like shallow depth of field to the nuances of different focal lengths. Whether it's the softness of an 18mm lens for a sweeping landscape or the intimacy of a close-up shot with a narrow focus, VO2 delivers visuals that reflect the creative intent behind the prompt.

Angles and camera movements are treated with equal care. VO2 doesn't simply position a virtual camera arbitrarily; it considers composition, perspective, and framing to ensure the output resonates with visual storytelling principles. The result is a level of polish that was once thought to be the exclusive domain of human cinematographers.

This integration of real-world physics and cinematic understanding positions VO2 as more than just a tool—it becomes a collaborator, enabling creators to produce visuals that are not only technically flawless but also emotionally resonant. It is this combination of realism and artistry that sets VO2 apart, making it an indispensable asset for anyone looking to push the boundaries of AI-generated visuals.

Google's VO2 isn't just about delivering visually stunning results—it's about doing so with the technical prowess required to meet the demands of modern creators. One of its most impressive capabilities is its ability to generate outputs in 4K resolution, a standard that has become synonymous with professional-grade content. For years, AI-generated videos have been plagued by limitations in resolution, often appearing blurry or pixelated when scaled for larger screens. VO2 eliminates this issue, producing visuals that maintain sharpness and clarity, even on the largest displays.

The significance of 4K resolution goes beyond aesthetic appeal. High-resolution visuals allow for greater flexibility in post-production, whether that involves cropping, zooming, or integrating AI-generated clips into larger projects without sacrificing quality. For filmmakers, marketers, or digital artists, this capability ensures that the content is not only visually compelling but also versatile enough to meet a variety of production needs.

VO2's technical advancements don't stop at resolution. One of its game-changing features is its ability to generate extended video sequences, stretching beyond the brief clips that earlier models struggled to produce. This leap is particularly important for creators working on projects that require longer, flowing visuals—be it a narrative film, an extended marketing campaign, or a music video. Previously, creators relying on AI tools were often limited by the short duration of generated clips, forcing them to piece together fragments that lacked continuity. VO2 addresses this by producing sequences that are not only longer but also seamless in their transitions, maintaining consistency in lighting, movement, and composition throughout.

This capability opens up a world of possibilities for creators. Imagine being able to generate a two-minute cinematic sequence that tells a coherent story, complete with dynamic camera movements, realistic lighting shifts, and lifelike character animations—all from a single prompt. The ability to create extended sequences also reduces the need for heavy editing or manual adjustments, saving time while delivering a polished final product.

These technical features underscore the practical value of VO2 for professionals across industries. Whether it's creating a visually stunning brand campaign or crafting a film with limited resources, VO2's high-resolution outputs and extended video capabilities ensure that creators are no longer constrained by the limitations of earlier AI tools. Instead, they have the freedom to focus on their vision, knowing that the technology can keep pace with their ambitions.

As AI-driven visuals become increasingly sophisticated, ethical considerations take center stage. The ability of tools like VO2 to generate hyper-realistic content raises questions about authenticity and potential misuse. One of the most pressing concerns is the creation of deepfakes—videos that manipulate reality in ways that can deceive viewers. Recognizing this risk, Google has integrated a Synth ID watermark into the outputs of VO2. This feature ensures that AI-generated content is identifiable, helping to maintain transparency and accountability.

The Synth ID watermark is not visible to the naked eye, which means it doesn't interfere with the aesthetic quality of the visuals. However, it can be detected through digital analysis, providing a reliable method to verify the origin of a video. This approach reflects Google's commitment to ethical AI development, striking a balance between empowering creators with cutting-edge tools and safeguarding against malicious applications. By embedding this watermark, Google takes a proactive step in addressing concerns about authenticity and trust in the age of AI-generated media.

Beyond ethical safeguards, VO2's potential is most evident in its wide range of applications. One of its early successes has been in the realm of YouTube Shorts, where creators are leveraging the tool to produce high-quality backgrounds and visual effects in record time. For content creators working under tight deadlines or with limited budgets, VO2 provides a solution that delivers professional-grade results without the need for expensive equipment or extensive post-production work. This accessibility is transforming how creators approach short-form content, enabling them to stand out in a crowded digital landscape.

Filmmaking is another area where VO2 shines. Independent filmmakers, in particular, often face constraints when it comes to achieving cinematic quality. VO2's ability to simulate realistic lighting, natural movement, and professional cinematographic details allows these creators to elevate their projects to a level that was previously out of reach. Whether it's crafting intricate visual sequences or enhancing a narrative with immersive effects, VO2 serves as a powerful ally in bringing creative visions to life.

In marketing, VO2's capabilities are equally transformative. Brands can use the tool to generate compelling visuals for advertisements, promotional campaigns, or product demonstrations. The ability to produce high-resolution, visually striking content quickly and efficiently is a game-changer for marketers looking to captivate audiences and communicate their message effectively. Moreover, the flexibility to generate extended video sequences means campaigns can feature cohesive storytelling, enhancing engagement and impact.

By addressing ethical concerns through measures like Synth ID and showcasing versatility across diverse applications, VO2 positions itself as a tool that not only advances creativity but also aligns with responsible innovation. Its ability to empower creators while maintaining safeguards ensures that the technology can be embraced confidently, unlocking new possibilities across industries.

In a rapidly evolving field of AI-generated visuals, VO2 distinguishes itself by addressing many of the challenges that have hindered other tools, including its closest competitor, OpenAI's Sora. While both platforms represent significant strides in AI technology, their differences highlight why VO2 is increasingly becoming the preferred choice for creators seeking both quality and reliability.

One of the most notable aspects of VO2 is its unparalleled attention to real-world physics. Unlike earlier models or even Sora, which sometimes struggles with unrealistic movements or lighting inconsistencies, VO2 generates visuals that feel authentic. Its ability to understand how light interacts with objects, how shadows should fall, and how movement aligns with gravity and weight gives its outputs a natural quality that creators value. This understanding is critical for applications where realism is not just a preference but a requirement.

Sora, on the other hand, has earned praise for its ability to generate detailed visuals from text prompts, making it accessible and intuitive for users. However, its results can be inconsistent. Many users have reported physics-defying moments or anatomical oddities, such as characters with extra fingers or awkward joint movements. These flaws, while occasionally amusing, undermine the tool's ability to produce polished, professional-grade content. VO2 avoids these pitfalls by refining its model to minimize such errors, ensuring outputs that are both technically accurate and visually pleasing.

Cinematography is another area where VO2 takes a commanding lead. Its understanding of camera angles, lens effects, and depth of field allows it to deliver outputs that align with professional filmmaking standards. For instance, when a creator specifies a close-up with a shallow depth of field, VO2 executes the request with precision, producing results that feel like they were shot on a high-end camera. Sora, while innovative, lacks the same level of cinematic detail, often requiring additional adjustments in post-production to achieve comparable results.

Resolution and length are also key differentiators. VO2's ability to produce 4K outputs and extend sequences to minutes in length gives creators the flexibility to work on a broader range of projects, from short-form content to longer narratives. Sora, in contrast, has been more limited in both resolution and sequence duration, making it less suitable for creators aiming for high-end or extended productions.

These distinctions are not merely technical—they reflect the practical needs of creators who rely on these tools to meet the demands of their audiences. VO2's consistent ability to deliver realistic, cinematic-quality outputs sets it apart as a reliable partner for professionals and hobbyists alike. While Sora remains a strong contender and a testament to OpenAI's ingenuity, VO2's combination of realism, precision, and versatility positions it as the tool of choice in the competitive landscape of AI-driven visuals.

Chapter 3: ImageN 3 – Elevating AI-Generated Art

VO2 represents a significant leap forward in AI-generated visuals, refining its capabilities to address the limitations of earlier versions. One of its most notable advancements is its enhanced ability to adhere to specific styles and textures, delivering results that are not only accurate but also richly detailed. This improvement reflects a deeper understanding of the nuances that make each visual style unique, from the grain of a photorealistic image to the soft, fluid brushstrokes of an impressionist scene.

Adherence to style is no small achievement in the world of AI-generated content. Previous iterations often produced results that missed the mark, blending elements awkwardly or failing to replicate the intricacies of a desired aesthetic. Textures, in particular, posed a challenge. For example, a model attempting to generate a lifelike metallic surface might instead produce something flat or overly simplified. VO2 overcomes these hurdles, capturing even the finest details with precision. Metallic surfaces gleam with realistic reflections, while natural materials like wood or stone carry a tangible sense of depth and texture.

Another area where VO2 excels is its ability to handle an expansive range of artistic styles. It goes beyond the generic or one-dimensional outputs of older models, offering creators the flexibility to generate visuals that align with their unique vision. Whether the task is to create a photorealistic scene that mimics the clarity of a high-resolution camera or an anime-inspired sequence bursting with vibrant colors and expressive characters, VO2 delivers with remarkable fidelity. The tool's versatility extends to impressionist and abstract styles as well, allowing for playful experimentation and creative exploration.

This broader stylistic range isn't just about aesthetic diversity—it's about empowering creators to tell stories in their own voice. A marketing team might use VO2 to produce sleek, photorealistic product visuals for a high-tech campaign, while an independent artist might opt for an impressionist approach to evoke emotion or nostalgia. For storytellers, the ability to switch seamlessly between styles opens up new avenues of creative expression, ensuring that the medium complements the message.

These improvements reflect Google's commitment to pushing the boundaries of what AI can achieve in the creative space. By focusing on enhanced style adherence and expanding the range of options available to creators, VO2 establishes itself as a tool that doesn't just respond to prompts—it understands and elevates them. This level of refinement is what sets VO2 apart, making it an invaluable resource for professionals and enthusiasts alike.

One of VO2's defining strengths lies in its precision and attention to detail, qualities that elevate it far beyond earlier iterations of AI visual tools. Its advanced capabilities in replicating lighting and textures bring an unparalleled level of realism to its outputs, enabling creators to achieve results that feel both authentic and immersive. Whether it's the warm glow of sunlight filtering through a forest or the intricate play of reflections on a polished surface, VO2's understanding of light dynamics adds depth and richness to every frame. This ability to mimic the subtleties of real-world environments makes it an invaluable tool for creators seeking to captivate their audiences.

Texture replication, too, has reached new heights with VO2. The tool can faithfully reproduce the tactile qualities of various materials, from the softness of fabric to the ruggedness of stone. This precision allows creators to craft visuals that evoke not just a sense of sight but also an imagined sense of touch. For advertising and branding, where the goal is often to make products as appealing and lifelike as possible, these capabilities are a game-changer. VO2 enables marketers to showcase their products in stunning detail, ensuring that every surface and texture is rendered to perfection.

Beyond commercial applications, VO2 is also proving to be a powerful ally in artistic experimentation. Artists can push the boundaries of their creativity, combining realistic textures with imaginative lighting to produce visuals that are both grounded and fantastical. This versatility allows for an endless range of possibilities, from photorealistic scenes to abstract compositions that challenge conventional norms.

The accessibility of VO2 further amplifies its impact. Through its integration with Google's Image FX platform, the tool has been rolled out to over 100 countries, ensuring that creators worldwide can harness its capabilities. This global reach democratizes access to cutting-edge technology, enabling individuals from diverse backgrounds and industries to participate in the AI-driven creative revolution. By removing geographical and financial barriers, VO2 helps level the playing field, empowering creators regardless of their resources or location.

Ethical considerations remain at the forefront of VO2's development, with measures like the Synth ID watermark ensuring that AI-generated content is both identifiable and trustworthy. This invisible watermark doesn't compromise the aesthetic quality of the visuals but provides a crucial layer of transparency, allowing users to distinguish between AI-generated and human-created content. In a world increasingly concerned with authenticity and the potential misuse of AI, this commitment to responsible innovation sets a standard for others in the field.

Together, these advancements in precision, accessibility, and ethics position VO2 as more than just a tool—it's a bridge to a future where creativity knows no bounds, yet remains firmly rooted in responsibility. Its applications span industries and artistic endeavors, and its global rollout ensures that its impact is as wide-reaching as its potential.

Chapter 4: Whisk – A Creative Twist on Image Generation

Whisk introduces a novel approach to AI-driven visual creation, shifting the focus from traditional text prompts to a more intuitive and visual method of input. Instead of relying on descriptive language to communicate their ideas, users can now upload images that serve as the foundation for generating new visuals. This process allows creators to work directly with visual elements—an image of a character, a specific setting, or even a unique texture—and use them as building blocks to craft something entirely new.

The power of Whisk lies in its ability to blend multiple image inputs into a cohesive and imaginative output. A user might upload a cartoon image of an animal, a photograph of a scenic background, and an abstract painting style. Whisk then combines these elements, creating a seamless fusion that reflects the essence of all three. The result is a creative output that retains the individual characteristics of each input while transforming them into a unified, visually compelling composition. This approach simplifies the creative process, making it accessible even for those who may struggle with articulating their ideas through words.

At the core of Whisk's functionality is Google's Gemini model, a sophisticated AI system designed to analyze and interpret input images. Gemini breaks down each visual into its essential components, identifying details such as color schemes, textures, lighting, and shapes. It then generates a detailed internal description of these elements, which it passes on to the underlying engine powering Whisk. This analysis ensures that the resulting output reflects the nuanced characteristics of the inputs while adhering to the user's creative vision.

The integration of Gemini's analysis and Whisk's generation capabilities allows for a remarkable degree of refinement. Users are not limited to purely visual inputs; they can also include optional text prompts to guide the AI further, ensuring that the final product aligns with their specific goals. This hybrid approach strikes a balance between the precision of text-based input and the intuitive creativity of image-based input, making Whisk a versatile tool for creators across various disciplines.

Whisk's innovative approach is particularly valuable for brainstorming and rapid prototyping. By allowing users to remix existing visuals and experiment with combinations, it accelerates the creative process while maintaining a playful, exploratory feel. This makes it an ideal tool for designers, artists, and marketers who need to generate ideas quickly without sacrificing quality or originality.

In essence, Whisk redefines the way creators interact with AI, offering a more hands-on, visual approach to idea generation. By combining the analytical power of the Gemini model with the flexibility of image-based inputs, it opens up new possibilities for creativity, breaking down traditional barriers and empowering users to experiment and innovate with ease.

Whisk's approach to simplifying creativity represents a fundamental shift in how AI can support and inspire creators. By allowing users to rely on image inputs rather than text-based prompts, it streamlines the process of generating visuals, making it accessible to a broader audience. For those who find crafting precise or descriptive text prompts challenging, Whisk removes the barrier of language, enabling them to focus entirely on their vision. This simplicity transforms Whisk into a tool not just for experts but for anyone with an idea to explore.

One of Whisk's most powerful applications is its use in brainstorming and rapid prototyping. In creative industries, the ability to experiment quickly and iteratively is often the difference between a good idea and a groundbreaking one. With Whisk, users can upload multiple image references—perhaps a photograph of a landscape, an abstract painting, and an intricate texture—and see how these elements combine to create something new. This capability makes it ideal for early-stage concept development, whether for film, advertising, game design, or art projects. The quick generation of visuals allows teams to refine ideas on the fly, fostering a collaborative and iterative workflow.

Whisk also excels at blending multiple image styles to produce unique results that might not have been conceived otherwise. Imagine uploading an impressionist painting, a surrealist composition, and a high-resolution photograph—Whisk can merge these styles, creating an output that carries the essence of all three while still feeling cohesive. This ability to hybridize aesthetics is particularly valuable for creators looking to push the boundaries of their medium, offering a playground for innovation and experimentation.

The implications of Whisk's user-friendly approach extend far beyond professional use. Its accessibility opens the door to creators who may have been excluded by the technical or linguistic demands of traditional AI tools. Hobbyists, students, or even individuals who simply want to explore their creative potential can engage with Whisk without needing specialized knowledge or training. This democratization of AI creativity ensures that more voices can participate in shaping visual storytelling, enriching the diversity and scope of creative output.

Moreover, Whisk's emphasis on experimentation expands the possibilities for what can be achieved with AI. It encourages users to think beyond conventional boundaries, allowing them to explore combinations and concepts they might not have considered before. This freedom to experiment, paired with the ease of generating results, fosters an environment where innovation thrives.

In essence, Whisk simplifies the act of creation, making it more intuitive and inclusive. Its ability to generate unique visuals through the combination of multiple styles, paired with its accessibility for users of all skill levels, positions it as a tool not just for creating visuals but for sparking ideas. By lowering barriers and expanding possibilities, Whisk invites everyone to participate in the creative process, reshaping how we think about art, design, and storytelling.

Chapter 5: The Competitive Landscape

OpenAI's Sora has made waves in the AI-driven visual space, showcasing remarkable capabilities that highlight the potential of this rapidly evolving technology. At its best, Sora delivers awe-inspiring results, transforming simple text prompts into intricate and highly detailed video sequences. Its intuitive interface and ability to interpret user input have made it accessible to creators across a variety of disciplines, solidifying its place as a significant player in the AI creativity landscape.

One of Sora's most notable strengths is its versatility. The platform can generate a wide range of visuals, from surreal, dreamlike sequences to grounded, realistic environments. Its ability to interpret text and transform it into vivid imagery allows creators to bring abstract concepts to life, making it a valuable tool for storytelling, conceptual work, and artistic experimentation. Sora's outputs often showcase stunning visuals that demonstrate a sophisticated understanding of texture, color, and composition.

However, while Sora's capabilities are undeniably impressive, its results can sometimes be inconsistent, revealing the challenges of pushing the boundaries of AI technology. A common issue lies in its handling of physics and movement. While some generated sequences appear natural and lifelike, others falter, displaying physics-defying visuals that break immersion. Characters might move in ways that feel awkward or unnatural, or objects might behave in ways that defy the laws of gravity, detracting from the overall realism of the scene.

Anatomical accuracy is another area where Sora occasionally struggles. Outputs have been known to include oddities such as characters with extra fingers, misshapen limbs, or facial features that don't align properly. While these quirks are often small, they can disrupt the illusion of believability, especially for creators aiming for polished, professional-grade results. These inconsistencies make Sora less reliable for projects where precision and realism are paramount, requiring users to invest additional time in editing or regenerating outputs.

Despite these weaknesses, Sora remains a powerful tool with immense potential. Its ability to generate visuals that capture the imagination has made it a favorite among creators willing to navigate its quirks. For projects that prioritize creativity over strict adherence to realism, Sora excels, offering outputs that are unique and thought-provoking.

As AI technology continues to advance, it's likely that many of Sora's current limitations will be addressed. OpenAI's commitment to innovation suggests that future iterations of the platform will build on its strengths while minimizing its weaknesses. For now, Sora stands as both a testament to how far AI has come and a reminder of the challenges that remain in perfecting these groundbreaking tools. Its journey highlights the delicate balance between technological ambition and the pursuit of consistency, a balance that defines the competitive landscape of AI-driven creativity.

The competitive landscape of AI-driven visual tools is becoming increasingly dynamic, with a host of players striving to carve out their niche. Beyond the headline-grabbing innovations from Google and OpenAI, several other platforms are making significant contributions to the field, each bringing unique strengths and approaches to the creative process. Among these competitors, Runway ML, P Labs, and Luma AI stand out for their distinctive features and targeted applications.

Runway ML has established itself as a pioneer in AI-powered video editing and generation, with its Gen 3 Alpha Turbo model pushing the boundaries of what's possible in AI video creation. Known for its advanced controls and user-friendly interface, Runway ML allows creators to manipulate outputs with a level of precision that is rare in the industry.

The Alpha Turbo model introduces even faster processing times and enhanced output quality, making it a popular choice for professionals who value efficiency. Its integration into workflows for filmmaking, advertising, and social media content production demonstrates its versatility and appeal to a broad audience. However, while it excels in speed and usability, its visual outputs occasionally lack the cinematic polish that tools like Google's VO2 provide, leaving room for improvement in high-end applications.

P Labs' Pica 2.0 takes a different approach, focusing on customization and personalization. One of its standout features is the ability to incorporate user-provided characters into AI-generated videos, offering creators a level of creative control that is particularly appealing for projects requiring specific branding or storytelling elements. This customization capability makes Pica 2.0 a valuable tool for industries like animation, game design, and marketing, where consistency and character-driven narratives are key. While its specialization in this area sets it apart, Pica 2.0 is somewhat limited in its scope, making it more of a niche tool compared to the broader applications of VO2 or Sora.

Luma AI's Dream Machine represents another intriguing entry in the competitive space, particularly for its focus on accessibility and enterprise use. By partnering with AWS, Luma AI has been able to scale its tools and make them widely available to businesses looking to integrate AI into their production pipelines. Dream Machine emphasizes seamless collaboration and cloud-based processing, allowing teams to work together efficiently across different locations. Its applications extend beyond traditional creative fields into areas like education, training, and virtual reality, showcasing its adaptability. However, like many enterprise-focused tools, it may feel less approachable for individual creators or smaller teams, who may be deterred by its technical complexity or enterprise pricing structure.

Each of these competitors brings something unique to the table, reflecting the diversity of needs within the creative community. Runway ML's speed and usability, Pica 2.0's focus on customization, and Luma AI's enterprise scalability all address specific pain points, ensuring that creators have a range of options to suit their particular goals. While they may not yet rival the cinematic finesse or comprehensive capabilities of Google's VO2, their specialized strengths contribute to a richer and more competitive ecosystem, driving innovation forward and expanding the possibilities of AI-driven creativity.

Google's tools, VO2 and ImageN 3, have set a high bar in the competitive landscape of AI-generated visuals, earning widespread acclaim for their unparalleled realism, advanced user control, and strong preference among creators. While competitors like OpenAI's Sora, Runway ML, and P Labs bring noteworthy innovations to the field, Google's offerings consistently stand out for their ability to deliver professional-grade results with a blend of precision and versatility.

At the heart of VO2's appeal is its mastery of realism. Unlike tools that sometimes falter with physics-defying movements or awkward anatomical details, VO2 generates visuals that feel grounded in the real world. From lifelike facial gestures to the fluidity of character movement, VO2 ensures that every element behaves naturally, aligning with the principles of physics and human anatomy. This attention to detail extends to lighting, where the tool excels at capturing subtle shifts and reflections, creating atmospheres that resonate emotionally and visually.

ImageN 3, Google's flagship for image generation, takes this focus on realism to new heights by delivering outputs that are richly textured and highly detailed. Its ability to replicate diverse styles with fidelity—whether photorealism, impressionism, anime, or abstract art—gives it an edge over competitors. Unlike earlier AI models that struggled with adherence to specific artistic directions, ImageN 3 achieves an uncanny ability to translate prompts into visuals that align closely with user expectations, whether they are looking for vibrant realism or imaginative abstraction.

Control is another area where Google's tools excel. VO2's understanding of cinematic principles, including depth of field, camera angles, and lens effects, empowers creators to produce outputs that feel intentional and polished. This capability is invaluable for filmmakers and marketers who rely on precise visual storytelling to convey their message. Similarly, ImageN 3's ability to adapt to a wide range of styles and textures provides creators with the flexibility to tailor outputs to their exact needs, whether for advertising, branding, or artistic experimentation.

These technical strengths translate into a clear preference among users. Human evaluators consistently rate outputs from VO2 and ImageN 3 higher than those from competitors, citing better alignment with prompts and a more polished overall look. This user preference isn't just about technical superiority—it reflects the tools' ability to meet the creative and emotional needs of their audience, fostering trust and reliability.

What truly sets Google's tools apart, however, is their combination of cutting-edge technology with ethical safeguards. Features like the Synth ID watermark ensure that AI-generated visuals are identifiable, addressing concerns about misuse while maintaining the integrity of the creative process. This attention to responsible innovation reinforces Google's position as a leader not only in technical capability but also in ethical AI development.

In comparison, while tools like OpenAI's Sora and Runway ML's Gen 3 Alpha Turbo offer compelling features, they often lack the consistency and finesse that Google's tools provide. VO2 and ImageN 3 not only match the demands of professional creators but also anticipate their needs, delivering results that are not just visually stunning but also practical and reliable. This combination of realism, control, and user trust ensures that Google remains at the forefront of AI-driven creativity, setting a benchmark for the industry.

Chapter 6: Challenges and Limitations of AI Visual Tools

Despite the impressive advancements in AI-generated visuals, even the most sophisticated tools like Google's VO2 and ImageN 3 are not without their limitations. While these tools excel in many areas, their occasional quirks remind us that AI, for all its capabilities, has yet to fully replicate the nuance and artistry of human creativity.

One persistent issue lies in the occasional anomalies present in AI-generated outputs. For example, characters might appear with extra fingers, misplaced limbs, or facial features that don't align properly. These quirks, while less frequent than in earlier models, still occur, often breaking the illusion of realism that the tools strive to achieve. Similarly, movements can sometimes feel slightly off, with awkward physics or unnatural transitions that detract from the flow of a scene. These errors, though less common in Google's tools compared to others, highlight the challenges of achieving flawless accuracy in the complex interplay of anatomy, physics, and motion.

These imperfections underscore the broader difficulty of replacing human creativity. While AI tools like VO2 and ImageN 3 are remarkable in their ability to generate visuals, they lack the intuitive understanding and emotional depth that human creators bring to their work. Creativity is more than the sum of technical elements like lighting, movement, and texture—it is about intention, storytelling, and the ability to evoke emotions in ways that resonate deeply with an audience. AI, for all its computational power, struggles to replicate this human touch.

This limitation becomes particularly evident in projects where artistic vision and subjective judgment are paramount. For instance, while AI can produce a visually stunning background or a lifelike character, it cannot independently decide how these elements should interact to create a compelling narrative. It relies on the guidance of human creators to provide context, purpose, and meaning, serving more as a tool for execution than a source of inspiration.

Moreover, AI's dependence on training data introduces its own set of challenges. The models are only as good as the datasets they learn from, which means they can sometimes reflect biases or gaps in the data. This can result in outputs that are less inclusive or fail to capture certain cultural or artistic nuances, further emphasizing the need for human oversight and input.

Despite these limitations, it is important to recognize that AI is not meant to replace human creativity—it is designed to enhance it. Tools like VO2 and ImageN 3 excel at automating repetitive tasks, accelerating workflows, and generating ideas, freeing creators to focus on the conceptual and emotional aspects of their work. Rather than viewing these tools as substitutes, they are best seen as collaborators, extending the reach and possibilities of human creativity while still relying on the unique insights and imagination of their users.

In this evolving partnership between humans and AI, the imperfections of these tools serve as a reminder of their current role: to assist, not replace. As the technology continues to improve, it will likely address many of these quirks, but the essence of creativity will remain firmly in human hands, guided by emotion, experience, and a uniquely human understanding of the world.

As AI tools continue to gain traction in the creative world, they face a fair share of skepticism from artists and filmmakers who question their role in the artistic process. While the technology's potential is undeniable, many in the creative community are wary of its impact, citing both technical shortcomings and broader ethical concerns.

Criticism often stems from instances where AI-generated visuals fail to meet professional expectations. Real-world examples, such as the controversial AI-generated trailer unveiled at the Game Awards, highlight the limitations of current technology. Viewers pointed out that the trailer felt hollow, with awkward movements and an uncanny, lifeless quality that broke the immersion. These moments of failure reinforce the belief among skeptics that while AI may excel at mimicking surface-level aesthetics, it lacks the depth and nuance needed to create truly compelling visual narratives.

For many artists, this concern goes deeper than technical glitches. Creativity is a deeply human endeavor, shaped by lived experiences, emotional expression, and cultural context. There's a fear that as AI tools become more prevalent, they may devalue the work of human creators or lead to a homogenization of art, where unique perspectives are overshadowed by machine-generated outputs. Filmmakers, in particular, worry about the erosion of craft in areas like cinematography and character development, where the subtleties of human decision-making are vital.

Compounding these concerns are the ethical risks associated with AI-generated content. One of the most troubling is the potential for misuse, particularly in the creation of deepfakes or other forms of false authenticity. Hyper-realistic visuals generated by AI can be weaponized to spread misinformation, manipulate public opinion, or harm individuals by fabricating events or statements that never occurred. The implications of such misuse are far-reaching, threatening trust in digital media and raising questions about accountability.

To address these issues, transparency has become a cornerstone of responsible AI development. Google's implementation of the Synth ID watermark is a significant step toward mitigating these risks. By embedding an invisible yet detectable marker in AI-generated visuals, Synth ID ensures that such content can be identified and traced, even if it appears indistinguishable from real-world imagery. This safeguard not only helps to prevent misuse but also fosters trust by enabling audiences to differentiate between authentic and AI-generated content.

Despite these measures, skepticism persists, fueled by the challenges of balancing innovation with ethical responsibility. Critics argue that transparency alone isn't enough—there must also be ongoing efforts to educate users and audiences about the capabilities and limitations of AI. This includes fostering a culture of accountability among creators and platforms, ensuring that AI is used ethically and with respect for the integrity of human creativity.

Ultimately, the skepticism surrounding AI in the creative community reflects a broader dialogue about the relationship between technology and art. While tools like VO2 and ImageN 3 are powerful allies for creators, their integration into the artistic process must be handled with care, respecting the unique contributions of human ingenuity while addressing the ethical challenges that accompany such transformative innovations. In this evolving landscape, transparency, collaboration, and a commitment to ethical practices will be key to bridging the gap between AI's potential and the creative community's concerns.

Chapter 7: The Future of AI Creativity

The future of AI-driven creative tools like VO2 and Whisk is set to be marked by broader accessibility and increased adoption across diverse industries. As these technologies evolve, they are likely to become even more integral to the workflows of filmmakers, marketers, and hobbyists, breaking down traditional barriers to high-quality content creation.

One of the most exciting predictions for tools like VO2 and Whisk is their continued expansion into global markets. Currently accessible through platforms like Google's Video FX and Image FX, these tools are designed with scalability in mind. As technology infrastructure improves and cloud-based processing becomes more affordable, the accessibility of these tools is expected to grow, reaching creators in regions that have historically faced challenges accessing cutting-edge technology. This democratization of AI creativity has the potential to unlock talent and innovation from previously untapped areas, enriching the global creative landscape.

Filmmakers, both independent and professional, are poised to be some of the biggest beneficiaries of this expanding accessibility. For independent creators, tools like VO2 offer a way to achieve cinematic quality without the need for expensive equipment or large production teams. The ability to generate high-resolution, physics-aware visuals opens doors for ambitious projects that might otherwise have been limited by budget constraints. Professional filmmakers, on the other hand, can integrate these tools into their workflows to accelerate production timelines, experiment with visual concepts, or enhance post-production with AI-generated effects.

In the marketing world, the adoption of AI tools like Whisk is expected to soar as brands seek new ways to captivate audiences. Whisk's ability to remix visuals and rapidly generate fresh concepts makes it an ideal tool for brainstorming and content production. Marketers can use these tools to create striking visuals for advertisements, social media campaigns, and promotional materials, all while maintaining a level of customization that aligns with their brand identity. The speed and efficiency offered by AI tools will also enable marketers to respond more dynamically to trends, crafting content that resonates in real-time.

Hobbyists and enthusiasts, too, are likely to embrace these tools as they become more accessible and user-friendly. For individuals exploring creative pursuits for personal enjoyment or passion projects, AI tools offer a level of polish and sophistication that was once out of reach. Whether experimenting with animation, crafting unique artwork, or dabbling in short-form video production, hobbyists will find these tools empowering, allowing them to express their ideas in new and exciting ways.

As adoption grows, these tools will also become increasingly integrated with other technologies, such as augmented reality (AR), virtual reality (VR), and interactive media. This convergence could lead to even more innovative applications, from immersive storytelling experiences to interactive marketing campaigns that engage audiences on entirely new levels.

The expanding accessibility and adoption of tools like VO2 and Whisk signal a future where creativity is not constrained by resources or technical expertise. Instead, these tools will continue to level the playing field, enabling creators from all walks of life to bring their visions to life with unparalleled ease and quality. As they evolve, they will not only transform how content is produced but also inspire a new generation of creators to explore the limitless possibilities of AI-powered creativity.

The broader implications of AI in creative industries are transformative, reshaping how content is conceptualized, developed, and delivered. Rather than serving as a replacement for human ingenuity, AI is increasingly positioned as a collaborator—a powerful tool that enhances creativity by automating labor-intensive tasks, sparking new ideas, and expanding the range of what is possible. This collaborative relationship between human creators and AI tools like VO2 and Whisk marks a significant evolution in the creative process.

By handling repetitive or technically demanding elements, AI allows creators to focus on the emotional and narrative aspects of their work. Filmmakers can dedicate more time to storytelling while AI handles the intricacies of lighting, motion, and visual effects. Marketers can develop bold, imaginative campaigns without being constrained by tight budgets or lengthy production timelines. For artists, AI serves as a canvas that responds dynamically to their ideas, enabling rapid experimentation and refinement.

This shift has profound implications for workflows and budgets across industries. AI tools streamline production, reducing the time and resources required to achieve professional-grade results. Independent creators and small teams, who often face significant financial constraints, can now produce content that rivals the quality of larger productions. For businesses, the cost-effectiveness of AI means more ambitious campaigns can be realized without sacrificing quality or creative vision. Additionally, the efficiency gained from AI-driven workflows frees up time for creators to explore new ideas and push their boundaries, fostering innovation.

Creative possibilities are also expanding at an unprecedented pace. Tools like VO2 and Whisk allow creators to experiment with styles, formats, and concepts that might have been too costly or time-consuming to explore previously. This democratization of creative technology is enabling a more diverse range of voices and perspectives to emerge, enriching the global creative landscape and challenging traditional norms.

Ongoing developments in AI technology are driving this revolution forward, with companies like Google and OpenAI leading the charge. Their relentless innovation ensures that AI tools are not only becoming more sophisticated but also more accessible. Google's focus on realism and cinematic detail in tools like VO2, coupled with OpenAI's advancements in text-to-video generation with Sora, highlights the competitive energy fueling rapid progress. These companies are continually refining their models to reduce errors, enhance user control, and push the boundaries of what AI can achieve.

The pace of AI evolution is staggering. With each iteration, tools become faster, more accurate, and more versatile, opening up new possibilities for creators. Innovations such as real-time rendering, expanded stylistic options, and seamless integration with other technologies like AR and VR suggest that the future of AI-driven creativity will be even more immersive and interactive. This rapid progress is reshaping the industry landscape, creating opportunities for both established professionals and emerging creators to experiment and thrive.

However, this rapid development also raises questions about the future of human creativity. While AI tools are collaborators, not replacements, their growing role in content production challenges creators to adapt and find new ways to distinguish their work. The evolving dynamic between human vision and machine execution will likely define the next era of creative industries, as creators learn to harness AI's potential while preserving the unique, human aspects of their craft.

In this transformative moment, AI is not just changing how content is made—it is redefining the possibilities of creative expression. Companies like Google and OpenAI are at the forefront of this movement, driving innovation that is reshaping the creative world and inspiring a generation of creators to embrace the limitless opportunities offered by AI.

Conclusion

The advent of tools like Google's VO2, ImageN 3, and Whisk signals the beginning of a new era in creativity—one defined by unprecedented possibilities and groundbreaking innovation. These technologies have redefined what creators can achieve, offering tools that are not just faster and more efficient but also capable of producing visuals that rival traditional methods in quality and detail. From VO2's cinematic precision to ImageN 3's mastery of artistic styles and Whisk's intuitive approach to remixing visuals, these tools have demonstrated their ability to revolutionize workflows and empower creators across industries.

At the heart of this transformation is the profound potential of AI to empower creators. By automating repetitive tasks and handling technical complexities, these tools free creators to focus on the core of their craft: storytelling, imagination, and emotion. Filmmakers can achieve cinematic-quality visuals without million-dollar budgets, marketers can deliver impactful campaigns in record time, and hobbyists can bring their ideas to life with a polish that was once unimaginable. This democratization of creative power ensures that more voices, from diverse backgrounds and perspectives, can contribute to the ever-evolving tapestry of global creativity.

Yet, with great power comes great responsibility. The rise of AI in creativity also calls for a careful balance between technological advancement and ethical integrity. Tools like Synth ID demonstrate that transparency and accountability are not just options but necessities in this rapidly advancing field. As creators embrace these tools, they must also consider the implications of their use—ensuring that the outputs are honest, inclusive, and respectful of the craft's traditions and potential.

This is not just a moment for passive observation; it is a time for active exploration and engagement. The tools are here, their capabilities growing with every iteration, and the opportunity to redefine creativity is open to everyone willing to step forward. Whether you're a seasoned professional, a budding artist, or simply someone curious about the possibilities, now is the time to explore what these tools can do. Experiment, innovate, and push boundaries—but do so thoughtfully, understanding both the potential and the responsibility that comes with wielding such power.

As we look to the future, the question remains: How will AI shape the world of creativity? Will it simply enhance human ingenuity, or will it redefine the very essence of what it means to create? The answer lies not in the tools themselves but in how we choose to use them. This is your moment to be part of this transformative journey, to embrace the possibilities, and to leave your mark on this new era of creativity. The future of art, storytelling, and imagination is being written today—what role will you play?

www.ingramcontent.com/pod-product-compliance
Lightning Source LLC
Chambersburg PA
CBHW070411230526
45471CB00006B/2753